The Flag

Georgia Beth

The flag shows that people stand together.

There is a stripe for
each of the first states.

There is a star for
each state today.

Some of the stripes are red.

Some of the stripes are white.

Think and Talk

How do these people feel about the flag?

The stars are white too.

The stars are on a field of blue.

You can feel proud
when you see the flag.

You can raise it high.

You can put your
hand over your heart.

You can say the pledge.

You can sing the anthem.

The country changes
and grows.

The flag
waves on.

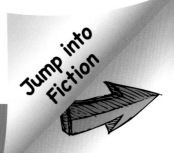

Sam and the Flag

Sam likes the flag.

He always looks for it.

He stands tall when he
sees it.

Civics in Action

There are rules for the flag. People want to take care of it.

1. Learn the flag rules.

2. Help an adult raise the flag.

3. Put your hand on your heart. Say the pledge.